Please return this book on or before the date shown above. To renew go to www.essex.gov.uk/libraries, ring 0845 603 7628 or go to any Essex library.

Essex County Council

Mark Reed

2016

The house buying process as it currently stands across the UK has a bewildering array of variation in the way the process takes place and whom is involved. How it works in Scotland is very different from England.

For the uninitiated, and even the experienced buyer. It can be a complex endeavour. So a simple understanding of the process and it's component parts may help smooth the path for those who are considering making the change.

The one aspect which remains fairly constant is that of obtaining mortgage funding. Therefore the purpose of this little book will be to provide further insight into the that part of the process .

Section one

Lending requirements
Loan types
Interest rates
Repayment vehicles.

Section Two

Life insurance

Mortgage Schemes

The costs incurred in the process of house purchase
One off payments and ongoing payments, to whom these are paid and for what reason they are incurred

Section One

Lending requirements

House purchase is frequently the biggest, and most stressful transaction we ever undertake. Sadly very few people are in the position of being able to make a cash purchase. Therefore some form of lending will be required.

Prior to any form of lending taking place, the potential borrower will go through an in depth interview process. The obvious reason for this is so the lender can assess whether the borrower is an acceptable risk for mortgage lending.

Not only is the prospective borrower assessed, but the lender will also assess the property itself to make sure that is also an acceptable risk.. it will undertake a series of requests for information. On the basis of that information, the lender will make it's decision to accept or decline either risk.

Borrower requirements

Income references
The are simply for proof of income, usually as follows
Employed people: Payslips over a 3-4 month period plus a P60 showing previous years income.
Self employed people: Business accounts over a 3-4 year period.

The lender may often request an employers or accountants reference to confirm the data on the previous documents.

Reasons, Lenders use a series of income multiples to gauge lending limits. If a single income is to be used, then they may use 3 times single income. There are cases of 4 and 5 times single incomes being used. see example below

Example 1

References confirm main income as £15.000 per annum.
Lender has a 4 times single income option.
Maximum loan will be £60.000.

There may be two incomes to be taken into account, in which case the lender may have a joint multiple of 3 times the main or higher income and one of the lower income.

References confirm a main income of 15.000 plus a second income of £5000. 3 times the main will be £45.000 plus one of the £5.000. Maximum loan will be £50.000.

These references also confirm details such as length of employment and job status: permanent or temporary.

Credit Searches

Every person who uses a credit/debit card, takes out a credit agreement will have a credit history. This history is preserved on a computerised data base, and is accessible to interested parties. Access can be gained online via specific outlets. Many companies have direct access via a dedicated link. The objective of this search is ascertain if there is existing debt, and the status of past debt. Good or bad. Good debt, well managed and either, being paid or been paid in accordance with the debt agreements.
Bad debt, non payment, arrears etc.

Outstanding loans

These are simply unexpired loans which the borrower is still in the process of paying off. The lender will be looking at the monthly cost and time over which the loan has to run. The lender may, depending on the loan details, deduct the annual cost of the loan from the borrowers annual income. Thus effecting the amount of capital it will lend.

County Court Judgements.

Most lenders take a fairly negative view to these. It basically shows a payment problem which has been subject to legal proceedings. These can be issued on individuals or business by institutions which take the dispute to the county courts. The courts ruled in their favour and issue the CCJ. This will basically stay on record until satisfactorily resolved. Either by full payment or a satisfactory offer

Once cleared the court will issue a certificate to confirm the fact.
In reality these can be very difficult to clear.

Proof of residency

This is documentation which confirms the individual lives at a specific location. The normal acceptances for these were utility bills bank or mortgage statements. However in some cases Passports, driving licenses or forms of specific ID are now being asked for. The credit check can also be used to ascertain proof of residency by checking voters roll records.

Lenders Reference.

These are taken up on borrowers who have an existing mortgage.

The lender is once again looking for consistency of payment. Should there be issues then clarification will be sought.

Landlords and Tenancy reference

Similar in context to the lender reference. Should the borrower live in rented accommodation. The lender will require a landlords reference to both confirm regularity of payment and proof of residence. Once again if payment problems exist clarification will be sought.

Bank Reference

Depending on requirements the lender may request one of these. It will be used to assess how the account is conducted, To basically ensure the income is going into the account and there are no issues with over draughts or lack of funds.

Property Requirements.

The lender will require details of the property on which the loan is to be secured, so it's condition will be assessed in a similar way.

Surveys, there are basically three types, with a few variations thrown in. They vary tremendously in both price and the information provided

Report and Valuation Survey

This is the basic form of survey. it is simply an assessment of the condition of the property in order to provide a valuation for mortgage purposes. It will hint at any possible defects in the structure and list any remedial work that may be required to rectify those issues.

Homebuyers Survey

This is a more in depth examination of the property structure. It will ascertain if there are any structural problems, such as subsidence or damp, as well as any other unwelcome hidden issues inside and outside. But it doesn't look beyond the floorboards or behind the walls. It does include the report and valuation as part of the package.

Full Structural Report

This is the most comprehensive survey and is suitable for all residential properties. although better suited for older homes or homes that may need repairs. This type of survey provides detailed advice on repairs. It's very extensive, but it does not usually include a valuation.

Although this survey and can't look under floorboards or behind walls it should include the surveyor's opinion on the potential for hidden defects in this area. The surveyor should also provide information on potential repair options.

Which type of survey you commission is often a matter of advice, preference or just plain affordability.. Prices for these vary considerably depending on condition, location and even the property price. A general rule of thumb may be to have the homebuyers on a relatively new property. Anything which is old or has issues you go with the full structural.

Retentions

These are an issue and quite common. It is where a survey throws up a serious problem which requires immediate attention. An estimate made to cover the cost of this repair will be taken from the survey. Subsequently the lender will issue an offer, but hold back funds to cover the cost of the repairs. These funds will only be released when any remedial work has been completed.

Conditions

These are where a survey has shown up areas of concern and a further investigation may be required. As an example, evidence of damp/dry rot have been located and specialist timber and damp reports may be required.

Subsidence is a major issue, it's simply where the ground beneath or around the house begins to shrink and crack effecting the stability of the structure. If it's found then a full structural report will be required.

Down valuations

With the fluctuation in house prices over the years this has become an increasing problem. Simply stated the surveyor values the property at less than the asking price. This may be down to location, condition or just inline with local market conditions. The lender will only lend the amount that the valuation states.

Many of these issues will require close work with the people managing the sale, your solicitors and estate agency professionals.

This covers the lender requirements prior to any offer of funding being made.

Loans

Mortgage loans like all others consist primarily of two elements. These are the capital borrowed, and the interest payable on it.

The way the following loan types differ is in how the re-payments are managed.

Capital Repayment Loan.

More frequently known as a repayment mortgage, it works thus. The borrower receives money from the lender, which is paid back along with interest over a certain period of time. As per the illustration below

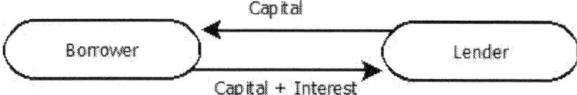

Interest Only Loans

These used to be the most common form of loan available and work thus. Payments are managed in what is essentially a three way split. The borrower receives money from the lender, but only pays back the interest portion of the loan. Not the capital borrowed. as per the illustration below.

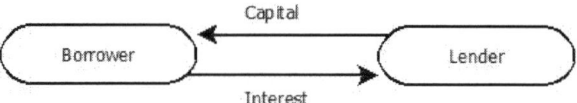

The third element in this set up is called the repayment vehicle. This can be any type of investment deemed as being acceptable for the purpose by the lender. These will be explained in further detail later.

The capital element of the loan is diverted into the repayment vehicle as per the illustration below.

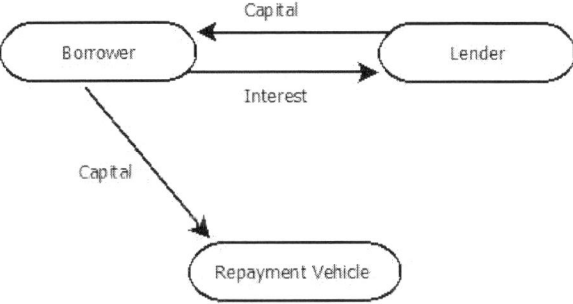

The idea being that over time, the amount paid into the repayment vehicle will generate interest, increase in value, and at the end of the term. Pay back the capital element of the loan. as per the illustration below.

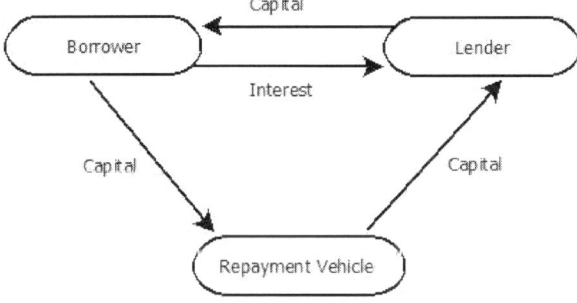

As previously stated the Interest only loan was subject to some serious issues. These will be clarified in the section on repayment vehicles.

Interest Rates

These are simply how much you are going to be charged for your borrowing, and are an integral part in the lending industry.
We all want to borrow money and pay the least possible price for doing so.

Variable rate

This is subject to interpretation, and can vary according to lending criteria. It is basically the current rate at which the lender is charging all borrowers. The term variable comes from the fact that the rate will fluctuate with market forces.

Many lenders offer specialised schemes which offer short term incentives to stimulate borrowing. Some are described below

Fixed rate schemes

These are simply where the lender offers lending at a fixed rate over a certain period of time. After which the scheme reverts to the variable rate applicable at that time.
Pros and Cons, useful in times of high interest rates, will keep the borrower locked into a lower fixed rate for a period of time.
If rates are fluctuating quickly, the borrower could end up stuck in a scheme where the variable rate has dropped below that of the fixed rate.

Capped rate schemes

Similar in organisation to a fixed rate scheme but different in application. Basically the rate is set to a value below the variable rate. If the variable rate remains higher, then your payments stay at the capped rate. However if the variable rate falls below the level of the capped rate. Your payments are adjusted to the lower level variable rate. Avoiding the pitfall of the fixed rate scheme. this is considered to be one of the best options available currently.

Deferred Schemes

Also referred to as an Adjustable Rate Mortgage: is a very complex animal which whilst it offers a degree of flexibility in early payments. It can cause serious issues in the later life of the loan if it is not fully understood. The following series of illustrations will show how it works.
For illustration purposes this example is worked over a 5 year period with interest rates rising at 1% per year. as per the graph below.

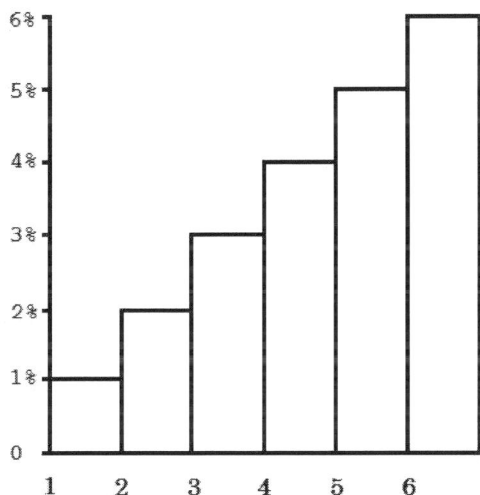

The graph shows payments rising over the first 5 years finishing at year 6 with the variable rate. During this time the borrower will have been paying interest at the rates quoted, BUT: The lender will have been charging interest at the variable rate. As per the illustration below.

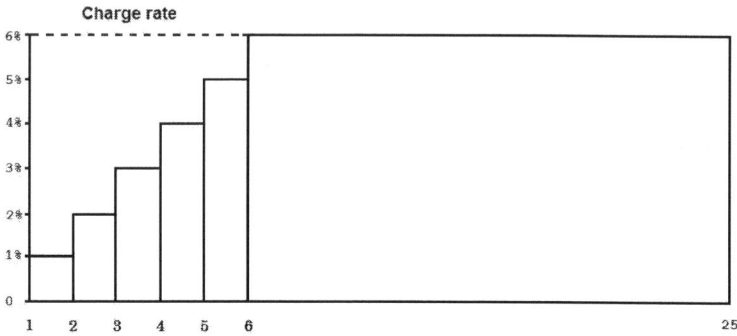

As can be clearly seen, there will be a shortfall between the early payments and the rate charged by the lender. This shortfall will be added to the remainder of the loan when deferred period expires. As per the illustration below.

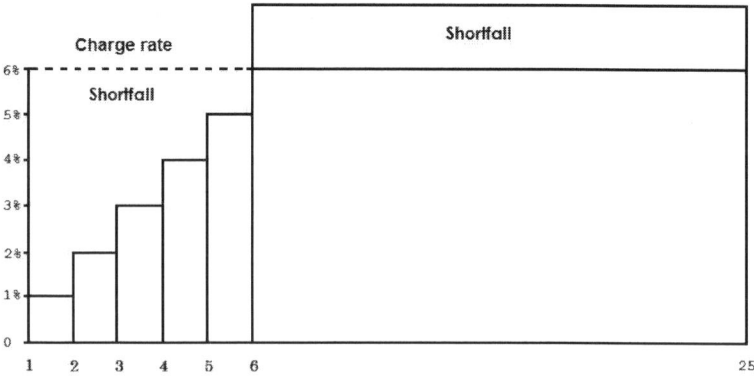

The difference between what was paid and what was actually charged is rolled up, or deferred, and added to the balance of the loan. Thus raising the original loan by that amount. It means the borrower ends up owing more than was originally borrowed.

Repayment Vehicles

These are investment methods available for use in mortgage borrowing.

These are as follows

Stock and Share portfolios
Bonds
Unit Trusts
ISA's
Savings
Pensions
Endowments

Stock and Share Portfolios

These are simply a collection of personal investments based on the ownership of company shares and stocks.

Investments Bonds

These are essentially a life insurance policy in which a capital lump sum is invested. They can be a fixed term investment. Over a specified amount of time, or open ended. Run till closed.

Unit Trusts

Here capital is invested into a Trust fund, managed by a Trust company. These are primarily open ended investment vehicles for long term growth capability.

Isa

Individual Savings Account, these are specialised savings accounts which offer tax relief on interest earned by capital in the account. The capital content is capped by the UK government to a specific amount which at the time of writing was £15.240.
Isa's come in two types, the cash Isa or the investment Isa. Either of these or a combination of both are acceptable as repayment vehicles.

Savings.

In certain cases cash held in a savings account may be an acceptable option. This varies between lenders.

Pensions

In certain cases a pension policy can be used as a payment vehicles. These are personal pensions only.
Company/Corporate pensions schemes are not accepted.

It works thus, when the pension term is complete, or the maturity date is reached. The personal pension can be taken in one of two ways.

One The whole fund can be taken as an Annuity or pension

Two A tax free lump sum of 25% can be taken, with the remainder of the fund being issued as an Annuity or pension.

Option two is used with a mortgage loan, as money from the tax free lump sum is used to pay back the loan. Whilst technically being a tax efficient method of payment, there is a serious drawback.
Pensions funds can only be taken on retirement and not before.
Therefore these are not suitable for buyers in their early years. Staying in one could lead to many more years in interest payments than would be the case with a conventional loan. These are certainly more suited to people in middle and later life as part of an investment or retirement plan.

Endowments

These used to be the most favoured form of investment method associated with mortgage lending. They are simply an insurance policy with elements of life cover and savings combined.

Apart from the cash Isa, which benefits from a fixed interest growth allowance. All of the above repayment options generate interest from exposure to market forces. That interest is generated in two ways, although both options can be used together in one investment method.

Unit Linked investments

Offered by life companies, investment is placed in a fund based on the value of assets owned by that company. Assets can be anything from property, commodities, Stocks/Shares and other investments.

This investment buys, units. A unit is essentially a single share in the fund, As the market fluctuates, the value of the fund rises and falls. each unit will rise and fall correspondingly.

The phenomenon is called **Pound Cost Averaging** and is a method that reduces exposure to fluctuating market conditions by using small investments over a long period of time. As opposed to a single large investment. it works thus. When the unit price is low, the premium buys more units but the value of the fund is low. When the unit price is high, the premium buys less units. However the value of the fund increases.

With Profits.

With this method, interest on the investment is generated on the performance of the company itself, not just the value of a specific funds assets. This type of investment was once favoured of the Assured/Mutual life companies, but now receives regular use across the industry.

It works thus, every year the life company will declare a policy bonus, this is called a reversionary bonus. These bonuses are issued annually throughout the life of the policy until the final year. They average between 3-5% of the fund value per annum

On maturity of the policy the company will issue a much larger bonus called the terminal or final bonus. It can vary from 25%-50% of the final value at maturity

Unlike unit linked investment where the fund value changes. Reversionary bonuses once declared on a with profits policy are fixed and cannot be changed.

The terminal bonus is paid at the discretion of the life company

The following illustration shows how it works.

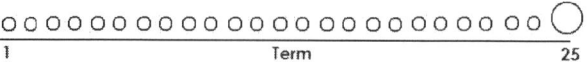

As can be seen, the annual bonuses are very small comparison to the final bonus. This investment method has a slower build up of capital in the earlier years. As can be seen the illustration below

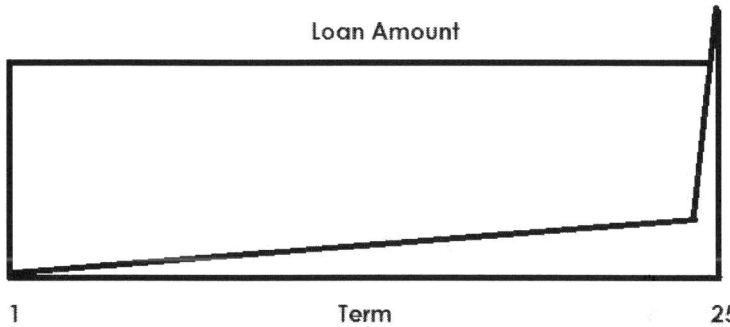

The main concern with all of these methods has been the failure to generate enough capital interest to cover the value of the original borrowing. Leaving many borrowers with insufficient funds to pay off their mortgages.

For this reason, interest only loans are strictly governed, and where they are used, are subject to very strict lending conditions.

Finally to end this section one very important and overlooked factor. It is the responsibility of the **BORROWER** to ensure that the repayment vehicle they are using is generating enough interest on the investment to pay the loan. Not the lender,

This ends section one

Section two

life Insurance

As unfortunate as it may sound, the prime reason for life insurance is to pay up debt in the event of death. There are basically two types of policy. One which is designed to do exactly that. The second has an extra investment option built into it.

Term Assurance

This comes with several options available, and is currently the prime form of life policy used with mortgage lending.

Level Term Assurance

This is simply where a set premium is paid, for a set sum assured. over a set number of years. Once maturity is reached that it is. The only pay out is on the death of the life assured. Used primarily on repayment mortgages.

Decreasing Term Assurance

The format works slightly differently here. The sum assured decreases over the term. In some cases the premium may also decline. Check to be sure of what your policy does. Once again the only payout is on the death of the life assured. Used again on repayment mortgages where the value of the loan is decreasing over time.

Increasing Term Assurance

Here the value of the sum assured actually increases over the term. Here again the premium may remain stable, or rise depending on the insurance provider. Once again payments will only be made on the death of the life assured. Used primarily on deferred or adjustable rate loans where the loan increases through the term.

Endowments

These were the primary method of security on interest only loans at one time. Unfortunately with the volatility of modern market conditions. Many of them never achieved the predicted level of growth. Leaving borrowers with insufficient investment to pay of their mortgage lending. These are much more expensive premium wise than the term assurance policies.

They are essentially a savings plan with a built in life cover element, and work thus. In the early years a large percentage of the premium is used to pay for life cover, with a small percentage channelled into an investment or savings element. As the term progresses more of the premium is placed into the investment, and less is paid on life cover. When the policy matures the savings on the policy will be passed back to the policy holder. It also pays out on the death of the life assured.

House Purchase schemes

These are essentially sales methods used by developers, builders, local councils and housing associations. To both attract and benefit potential buyers. For ease of understanding the term developer will be used to identify these organisation in the following examples

There are many variations of these options available, a sample of which are covered here

Equity value in a property

This is simply the difference between the value of the property and any mortgage taken out against it. The example below will explain this.

Purchase price of the property is £100.000
Mortgage secured against it is £75.000
The equity value is the difference between the two
£25.000

Shared Equity

Shared equity schemes work with the borrower receiving an equity loan to put towards buying a property. There are both government-backed schemes and also private sector schemes. With a government-backed scheme the equity loan comes from the government and developers who will lend up to 20% of the purchase price, depending on the particular scheme.. But the borrower must have a deposit of at least 5%, plus a mortgage of 75%.

Private sector equity loan schemes work in a very similar way but there will be differences such as, when the loan has to be paid and the size of the lender share if the property is sold.

Unlike the mortgage payment, The equity loan repayments can be paid as required, but it must be repaid in total after the full term. If the property is sold before then, the value of the loan would be deducted from the sale price. When the equity loan is repaid, it will reflect the market value of the property at that time, not a fixed cash amount. The example below shows how this works

The purchase price is £100.00: Purchaser raises £80.000: Equity Loan of 20% equates to £20.000

Property sold at £200.000, the equity payment will be 20% or £40.000

The opposite holds true if the property drops in price, so to will the equity value to be paid back Depending upon scheme types there may be additional fees incurred. Be sure to research the options available

Shared Ownership

Shared ownership is exactly that. The purchaser will part-buy and part-rent a property from a developer, allowing the option to take out a much smaller mortgage. Using this method, the purchaser can effectively buy a share of between 25% and 75% of a property value. then pay rent on the remaining share.

Depending on the scheme, the developers shareholding can be bought out, if the option is unavailable. The developers share remains constant and may only be redeemable on the sale of the property.

Deferred Purchase Schemes

Similar in application to the Shared equity scheme It is simply where the developer advances a capital sum.
That is over and above that raised by the borrower.
It is devised to act as a kind of bridging loan, to cover the difference between the capital raised by the purchaser, and the purchase price of the property. These kind of arrangements are normally worked between a developer and an estate agency for specific or high profile developments.
Terms and conditions will certainly vary depending on the scheme.

Right to Buy

This scheme has been around for a long time. Local Authorities are encouraged by law to offer housing to it's tenants at reduced prices. There are specific criteria which govern this type of sale. These are as follows. The buyer must have been a local Authority tenant for at least 3years. If the purchase is a house, discounts of 35 % are available. The same conditions are applicable to tenants of 4 and 5 years. However for each year of tenancy thereafter, an extra one percent is added to the discount. Up to a maximum of 70%.

With flats the tenancy criteria is the same, but the initial discount will be 50%. For each year after 5 years an extra 2% will be added up to the maximum of 70%

At the time of writing, There are cash ceilings in place as to the exact amount of discount given. It works thus properties outside of London receive up to a maximum discount of £77,900
Properties in London receive a maximum discount of £103,900
If a tenants discount reaches the 70% but exceeds either of these figures. Only these amounts will be issued.
The criteria governing these schemes may vary slightly between the various organisations charged with running them. Check the options carefully

Fees

This section deals with the fees which are incurred on house transactions. The majority are paid by the solicitor on completion of the sale. Those which are paid up front relate primarily to the lender.

The section will also be broken down to indicate single payments and ongoing payments.

The Lender

Valuation fees.

These are single payments made prior to the survey being done. Price is subject to the type of survey undertaken. and the purchase price of the property. The examples below give a rough guide

Mortgage report and valuation £150 plus
Housebuyers Report £350 to £950
Full Structural Report £500 to £1300

Admin/Arrangement Fees

These are primarily admin fees to cover costs incurred by the lender. When carrying out the information gathering stage prior to offer. They can include things like charges for credit searches, bank statements and reference requests, and are mostly paid for as and when required.

There may also be arrangement fees for specific mortgage schemes . If so, these can be either added to the loan as part of the offer or deducted from the loan as part of the offer.

Indemnity guarantee premium

This is essentially a single charge paid on what the lender deems as high risk borrowing. These can be either added to, or deducted from the loan at offer depending on the lender. They work as follows based on the loan to valuation.
The loan to valuation is the percentage loan offered against the valuation or purchase price.

Valuation of £100.000
Loan required £50.000
Percentage loan 50%

In general An indemnity guarantee will be charged where the lending exceeds 75% of the valuation. So based on the example above. Loans above £75.000 will incur an indemnity premium. Costs and applications for these will vary between lenders.

Redemption Fees

This is a charge which is levied by the lender if the mortgage is finished early, or moved to another lender. Such an example may be, where the purchaser wishes to raise additional funding by accessing some of the properties equity value. So the property is re-mortgaged with another lender. Obviously an after purchase expense that can easily be overlooked. Prices vary from lenders and amounts borrowed

Special reports

These can include things brought about by the surveys . Such as timber and damp reports, assessments on work required for subsidence or damaged structures etc.

Insurance

As well as life assurance on the loan, there will be risk which needs to covered on the property, so suitable buildings and contents insurance may well be required.

Estate Agency Fees

These are primarily commission based, and are calculated as a percentage of the purchase price. Between 1 and 2 percent. The figure is usually subject to agreement before the agent is instructed to act. This fee will be paid by the solicitor on completion of the purchase.

Arrangement Fees, in rare circumstances a charge may be made by the agent to cover initial costs. Any such charge would be agreed with the purchaser and paid up front.

Solicitors

All of these fees are paid after completion. This bill is the most expensive so requires a degree of explanation

The Estate agency fee will be collected and paid to the agent by the solicitor

Stamp duty: on registration of the sale, the purchaser may be eligible for stamp duty. The scales vary across different parts of the UK. The first example applies to England and Wales. This is paid to the Inland revenue by the solicitor. It is incurred where the purchase price exceeds £125.000 and works on a sliding scale as follows

Purchase price up to £125,000, Zero payment
Purchase price between £125,000 and £250,000, payment incurred at 2%
Purchase price above £250,000, payment incurred at 5%

In Scotland stamp duty comes into effect on purchases of £145.000 and works as follows

Purchase price up to £145,000, Zero payment
Purchase price between £145,000 and £250,000, payment incurred at 2%
Purchase price between £250,000 and £325,000, payment incurred at 5%
Purchase price between £325,000 and £750,000, payment incurred at 10%
Purchase price above £750,000, payment incurred at 12%

These were current at the time of writing

Solicitors

The solicitors fees are calculated on the work they actually do When the bill is drawn up, it will give a detailed breakdown of the costs and how they were incurred.

These then are the single payments fees as they occur throughout the process.

Lastly the ongoing payments

These are the most important, and are the ones which if not paid continuously could lead to repossession of the property

they are, in the case of a capital repayment loan. The capital and interest payments to the lender.

In the case of an interest only loan, the interest repayments to the lender. and the capital element into the repayment vehicle.

Two final things, you as the purchaser must ensure the repayment vehicle will be able to repay the loan. So monitor it regularly. If problems occur contact the lender.

Life assurance premiums, make sure these never get cancelled /stopped in anyway or form. When payment stops, the cover stops.

That then is where this document reaches a conclusion.

Whilst there is a lot of information presented here, it is not the complete process. That is way beyond the scope of this little book. Use what is here, in a way that inspires you to ask questions and get answers.

Happy House Buying

About the Author

The manuscript for this book was originally written back in the late 80's as a training manual and user guide for the industry professionals and public alike.

The original edits were located earlier this year 2016, and on examination it was found, that much of the information was quite specific and still very relevant. After much research into the industry as it is today. The information for this document was updated and reworked into a much smaller volume. So this little booklet on mortgage lending is the final result

Mark Reed spent 10 years in the insurance and mortgage world from the mid 80's to 90's firstly as an insurance consultant, moving into mortgages, then underwriting and debt consolidation. Finally running his own finance agency, specialising in debt management and consolidation, before moving on to explore his passion for music.

www.rmdmusic.com

www.dareyato.com

Mark Reed 2016

Made in the USA
Charleston, SC
17 February 2017